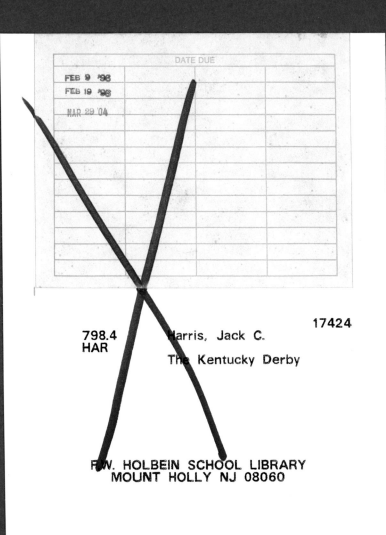

The KENTUCKY DERBY

Published by Creative Education, Inc.
123 South Broad Street, Mankato, MN 56001

Designed by Rita Marshall with the help of Thomas Lawton
Cover illustration by Rob Day, Lance Hidy Associates

Photography by Allsport, Amwest, Kinetic Corporation,
Globe Photos, Hillstrom Stock Photo, Wide World Photos

Printed in the United States

Library of Congress Cataloging-in-Publication Data

Harris, Jack C.
  The Kentucky Derby/by Jack C. Harris: edited by Michael E.
Goodman.
    p. cm.—(Great moments in sports)
    Summary: A history of Kentucky's famous horse race, which has
run continuously since 1875. Includes stories about some of its most
famous horses and jockeys.
    ISBN 0-88682-312-9
    1. Kentucky Derby, Louisville, Ky.—History—Juvenile literature.
[1. Kentucky Derby, Louisville, Ky.—History. 2. Horse racing—
History.] I. Goodman, Michael E. II. Title. III. Series.
SF357.K4H37   1989   89-23994
798.4′009769′44—dc20   CIP
                                                  AC

THE KENTUCKY DERBY

JACK C. HARRIS

CREATIVE EDUCATION INC.

The day of the Kentucky Derby begins quietly for the horses in the barns around Churchill Downs. The trainers try to keep their animals as calm as possible on this exciting day. Soon the horses will be moved to the grassy paddock where they will wait until it is time to be led onto the track for the race.

On any other day, for any other race, the horses would leave their barns and head for the paddock one by one. On Derby Day, they come together. As they near the twin spires of the Downs, they pass through a lane of people, all excited to see the Derby field. On any other day, no one would pay much attention to this activity. Derby Day is different.

Alysheba, like all thoroughbreds, can be identified by a unique tattoo.

The walk to the paddock is only seven minutes long, but it helps build the excitement of the race. It is the last time fans can see the horses up close before the race begins. The excited animals enter a small tunnel leading to the paddock where they are given a final inspection. The horses are officially identified by a tattoo on the inside of their upper lips. A Derby inspector checks these tattoos to make certain the proper horses are running.

The horses are assembled in the paddock a half-hour before the beginning of the race. Meanwhile, the jockeys are getting dressed and officially weighed. A jockey can weigh only 126 pounds if he is on a male horse, only 121 if he is on a filly. Twenty minutes before post time, the jockeys are sent to the paddock to join up with their mounts.

The jockeys meet up with their horses and form the post parade.

At approximately 5:15 p.m. on Derby Day, the horses are saddled and the paddock judge says, "Riders, up!" The crowd of more than 120,000 people becomes quiet as the band plays the Derby theme song, "My Old Kentucky Home," and the horses head for the track.

The quiet turns into applause and the cheering begins. The bright, silken jerseys of the jockeys add color to an already colorful day. Even the horses' names cause excitement. There's Clever Trevor, Flying Continental, Western Playboy, Hawkster, Shy Tom, Houston, Dansil, Faultless Ensign, Triple Buck, Sunday Silence, Irish Actor, Awe Inspiring, Wind Splinter, Northern Wolf, and the one favored to win, Easy Goer.

The horses head for the track to the strains of "My Old Kentucky Home."

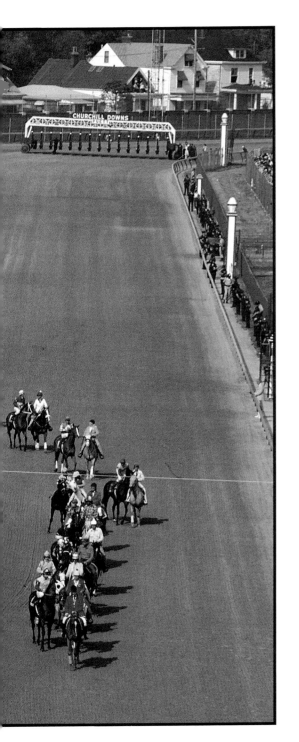

The horses line up at the starting-gate. The thousands in the grandstand hold their breaths. The millions of people watching on their televisions sit on the edge of their seats. It is the first Saturday in May, and it seems the whole world is watching this one horse race.

9

"H-h-h-here they come," says the track announcer.

It is now 5:25 p.m. The horses enter the track and canter up. With the beginning of the Derby only about fifteen minutes away, the horses will soon be loaded into the starting gate by assistant starters. These men and women enter the starting gate stalls and hold the horses' heads still until the final seconds before the start of the race.

The tension and excitement build. All the horses are ready. All the jockeys are prepared, leaning low on their mounts.

The three judges are ready too. In the stewards' stand, two of them watch the start with binoculars while the third watches on a pair of television monitors. After the race, the judges will closely view a replay of the race to make sure that none of the horses or jockeys interfered with each other. Other patrol judges are positioned near the five-eighths pole, the three-eighths pole, and just past the finish line.

The starter is in his stand. The announcer says, "It's post time!" At 5:50 p.m. the starter presses a button and the gates fling open. "There they go-o-o-o!" yells the announcer, and another running of the Kentucky Derby begins!

Heavy rains and cold temperatures the day before have made a mess out of the track, but the horses do not seem to mind. The thundering of their galloping hooves can still be heard on the muddy one-and-one-quarter-mile track. Those hooves seem to echo more than 100 years of horse-racing history at the Kentucky Derby.

THE RUN FOR THE ROSES

The Kentucky Derby has been run continuously at Churchill Downs racetrack, in Louisville, Kentucky, since the track was built in 1875. The one-and-one-quarter-mile-long race is limited to horses three years of age. Racing horses are considered to be in their prime when they are three. The Derby is a world-famous event today—it is the World Series or the Super Bowl of horse racing. But its beginnings in 1875 were pretty modest.

The first Kentucky Derby was held on May 17, 1875. Fifteen horses lined up at the starting gate to race for the $2,850 purse. (Winners today can earn more than half a million dollars.) One horse owner, H. Price McGrath, had entered two mounts in the race, Chesapeake and Aristides. McGrath had a plan in mind for winning the race. He wanted Aristides to set the pace and then let Chesapeake make a dramatic winning finish in the stretch. As the horses entered the backstretch, Aristides was ahead, with horses named Ten Broeck and Volcano right behind him. Chesapeake was in fourth place, ready to make his move for the win. However, when the moment came, Chesapeake was unable to take the lead. McGrath was horrified. He signalled the jockey riding Aristides to try for the win himself. Crossing the finish line to win the first Kentucky Derby, by a nose, was Aristides. McGrath probably breathed a sigh of relief as he welcomed the winning horse and jockey, and collected his prize money.

Forty years after the first Kentucky Derby, the event had become so successful that it was advertised as the greatest race in America. In 1915, Regret became the first filly to win the Derby, which also helped make the Kentucky Derby more successful and got the attention of more women racing fans. The Derby was now beginning to draw the attention of horse-racing fans throughout the United States.

Another important chapter in Derby history was made on the Derby's 50th birthday in 1924. People watching the Golden Jubilee race paid special attention to a horse named Black Gold, owned by Rosa Hoots, an Osage Indian. She and her husband, Al Hoots, owned a mare named Useeit who was the winner of several smaller races. Al believed that if Useeit was bred with the famous stud Black Toney, the offspring would be born with all the qualities needed to be a Derby winner.

Although Al died before the new horse was old enough to enter the Derby, his wife made his dream come true. She named the horse Black Gold after the oil that had made her rich. Black Gold won half of his first eighteen races but was considered only a long shot for a Derby win by most fans.

13

Eddie Arcaro (at right), along with Rosa Hoots, is one of the Derby's legends.

As the 50th Kentucky Derby progressed, it looked as if the fans were right. Black Gold was in the sixth position, boxed in by the other horses. Then, in the backstretch, Black Gold broke free and galloped furiously towards the leader, Chilhowee. The reporters and photographers pushed forward to see the exciting finish. The flashing of the cameras scared many of the horses, but not Black Gold. He kept coming and dashed across the finish line a mere half-length ahead of Chilhowee.

Rosa Hoots was proud of her horse, her husband, and her Indian heritage that day. She draped a blanket of roses over Black Gold as a reward. Hoots's action started a tradition, and Derby winners to this day are awarded a blanket of roses. The tradition inspired a radio announcer to nickname the Kentucky Derby, "The Run for the Roses," by which it is still known.

Today, more than sixty years later, with television coverage reaching around the world, the Kentucky Derby is more famous than ever. Each year, the eyes of most Americans and sports fans from around the world are all focused on Churchill Downs on the first Saturday in May.

Like Black Gold before him, Seattle Slew became a Derby champion in 1977.

GREAT WINNING TEAMS

Winning the Kentucky Derby takes teamwork. Each winning team consists of three partners—a horse, a jockey, and a trainer. Of course, the most important of these partners is the horse. A winning Derby horse has to love to run, take direction from the jockey and trainer, and concentrate on the race even when thousands of people are yelling in the stands, and a dozen or more other horses are crowding all around.

The horses, however, are not the only great athletes in the Derby. So are the jockeys. When the horses' hooves thunder around the final turn of Churchill Downs, very few people are thinking about the jockeys, but they are an important part of any Derby-winning team.

The horse runs the race, but the jockey has to guide the horse in the best direction in order to gain the lead. Only the best jockeys know the right moment to make the run for the finish line.

One of the greatest jockeys of all time, Willie Shoemaker, who has won four Derbies, once described what it takes to be a winning jockey. "Many elements distinguish the great rider from the average one—balance, intelligence, the ability to switch the whip from one hand to the other and back again, making the right moves most of the time, and a rapport [good relationship] with horses," he commented. "Most of the outstanding riders have all of these qualities."

Imagine being 4'1" and weighing 100 pounds and handling expertly a huge, 1,200-pound horse galloping at top speed! That takes quick thinking and strong hands and legs. These are skills that jockeys like Shoemaker develop only through long, hard training and plenty of athletic ability.

Willie Shoemaker has won four Kentucky Derbies.

Jones and Arcaro had just a few hours to develop their strategy for winning the race. They decided on a plan that would take advantage of the big horse's speed and spirit but would require lots of hard work on Arcaro's part. Arcaro was to take Hill Gail out at top speed from the start and then keep the horse from slowing down.

Hill Gail broke from the gate quickly and soon had a five-length lead. Spectators were shocked that Arcaro would risk tiring out his horse and losing the race. Arcaro leaned low over Hill Gail's back, almost burying his head in the horse's mane, his hands in rhythm with the horse's stride. Arcaro kept hammering at Hill Gail every time the horse seemed to falter, and the big horse kept going—all the way to the Winner's Circle. There, the winning team gathered and enjoyed a well-deserved round of applause.

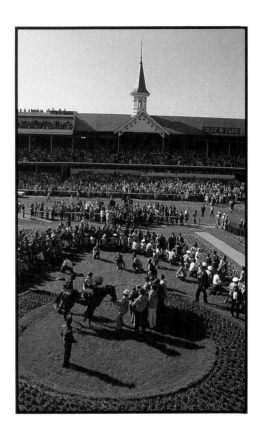

Derby champions parade to the Winner's Circle to receive their congratulations.

With the help of several great trainers and jockeys, there have been many magnificent horses who have risen to fame at the Kentucky Derby. Those who saw races before the turn of the century considered Hindoo to be America's greatest horse. In fact, old-timers used to say about a promising young horse, "He's all right, but he's no Hindoo." Hindoo ran in thirty-five races during his career. He won thirty, came in second three times, and was third in the other two. When he was a three-year-old in 1881, Hindoo won eighteen straight races, including the seventh Kentucky Derby.

In the grand tradition of Hindoo, Sunday Silence won the Derby in 1989.

After Hindoo came Exterminator, who was sent into the 1918 Derby as a "substitute." Exterminator was bought two weeks before the Derby as a workout partner for Sun Briar, the favorite in the race. Exterminator had not run a race in competition in over nine months. But Sun Briar looked sluggish in training before the Derby, and the owner and trainer decided to enter Exterminator instead. The big gelding was listed as a 30-1 underdog, but he won anyway on a very muddy track. The fans loved him and affectionately called him "Old Bones." "Old Bones" won fifty of 100 races during an eight-year career—not bad for a last-minute substitute.

The next year (1919), Sir Barton made history by becoming the first Triple Crown winner. The Kentucky Derby is the first leg of what has become known as "The Triple Crown." The Triple Crown is made up of three different horse races—the Kentucky Derby, the Preakness Stakes, and the Belmont Stakes. Only eleven horses in history have won the Triple Crown by being first in all three of these famous races.

Sir Barton was one of the few horses who debuted at the Kentucky Derby. This means he had never raced as a three-year-old horse before the Derby. All of the other horses in the 1919 race had run in other races prior to their Derby appearance. Sir Barton led for the entire race. From the moment the starting flag went down until the finish line, Sir Barton was ahead all the way.

Another great Kentucky Derby and Triple Crown winner was Whirlaway, who captured the "big three" races in 1941. Whirlaway was a great racer but was a little bit wild. He also had one problem: he tended to pull to the outside to avoid the other horses. His trainer, Ben A. Jones, who trained six Derby win-

ners in his career, had the answer. He devised a special one-eyed blinker that would let the colt see clearly only out of his left eye. Whirlaway would thus stay close to the rail and ignore the other horses in the race. With jockey Eddie Arcaro aboard and the blinker in place, Whirlaway whirled to an easy victory. Arcaro did not really direct the horse; he just hung on for dear life as the colt poured on the speed. Arcaro said of the horse: "He's the runningest son of a gun I ever sat on."

THE TOP THREE

Although the early days of the Derby saw some great champions, the period from 1948 to 1978 may have produced the three greatest horses of all time. A few years ago, some racing writers were asked to pick the most outstanding Derby winners. Their top three choices were Citation, Secretariat, and Seattle Slew—all Triple Crown Winners. There is an interesting story behind each great horse.

Citation and his brother Coaltown were two Calumet Farm horses trained by Ben A. Jones that ran in the 1948 Derby. Eddie Arcaro, who had ridden Whirlaway to victory, was aboard Citation. At first, Arcaro wanted to ride Coaltown, who was more spirited than his brother, but Ben Jones assured Arcaro that Citation was better. Jones was right.

Coaltown took the early lead and stretched it out to six lengths. Citation, however, was just getting warmed up. As Arcaro urged him on, Citation began to close the lead and then sailed by for an easy win. Citation kept winning after the Derby, too, taking nineteen of twenty races that year and racking up total winnings of more than $800,000. No horse had ever won $1 million before, but Citation accomplished that feat in the next three years. One veteran trainer who had watched more than fifty Derbies said, "There's never been a horse like Citation."

Unfortunately, that trainer never got to see Secretariat, who came along twenty-five years after Citation. During those twenty-five years, there were no Crown winners. Secretariat changed all that.

25

Only the most courageous and talented horses can achieve the Triple Crown.

Secretariat was a beautiful horse. He was golden-red, had three white stockings and a white blaze. Trainer Lucien Laurin trained the young horse and he won an astonishing seven of his first nine races. In 1972, a year before his Kentucky Derby appearance, he was named "Horse of the Year."

Secretariat was named "Horse of the Year" in 1972.

But people still had doubts about this handsome horse. In the Wood Memorial race, just before the 1973 Derby, Secretariat came in third, behind Angle Light and Sham. It was believed that he had a bad knee, and Sham became the Derby favorite. Owner Penny Tweedy and trainer Laurin were very disappointed. In 1972, they had won the Kentucky Derby with their horse, Riva Ridge. They were hoping to make history by being the first owner–trainer team to win two Derbies in a row.

On Derby Day, Sham hurt his mouth on the starting gate and a horse named Shecky Greene galloped out in front. For most of the race, Shecky Greene held the lead. Then, urged on by jockey Ron Turcotte, Secretariat began to move up on the outside. By the one-mile mark, Secretariat was second, only half a length behind Shecky Greene. The crowd was on its feet, the cheers almost drowning out the voice of the announcer as the two horses battled for the lead.

Secretariat crossed the finish line first, winning the race and smashing the Kentucky Derby speed record by finishing the one-and-one-quarter-mile distance in only one minute, 59-2/3 seconds.

Sham's trainer was not happy. He claimed that Secretariat had won only because Sham had injured his mouth. But Secretariat proved he really was a super horse just two weeks later at the Preakness. Racing against Sham again, Secretariat triumphed by two and a half lengths. After the Belmont, no one ever doubted Secretariat's greatness again. He won by an incredible thirty-one lengths, leaving poor Sham to come in dead last.

Secretariat was the first Triple Crown winner in a quarter of a century, and many people still believe he was the greatest horse of all time.

Four years later, another Triple Crown winner came on the scene. His name was Seattle Slew. He had sold as a yearling for only $17,500, but soon began an unbeaten career in which he won purses of several million dollars.

Seattle Slew battled to victory in the 1977.

Seattle Slew had a tough time in the Derby. He was banged so hard coming out of the starting gate that he almost fell to his knees. He courageously recovered, however, and still won by almost two lengths. Afterward, the great horse had an easy time in the Preakness and the Belmont Stakes to capture the Triple Crown.

THE GREATEST RIVALRY

One year after Seattle Slew's triumph, the 1978 Triple Crown races featured one of the greatest rivalries of all time. Facing off in the three races were Affirmed and Alydar. The two horses had some close battles as two-year-olds but didn't meet the next year until the Derby.

Racing fans around the world eagerly awaited the Derby. One of the reasons for their interest was Affirmed's jockey, Steve Cauthen. Cauthen had just turned eighteen, five days before the Derby. He was one of the youngest jockeys ever to race in the Derby. Cauthen had grown up in Kentucky and had first ridden a horse alone at the age of two. By the time he was seven, he was handling some horses that everyone else had trouble riding.

Alydar from Calumet Farm had captured lots of prep races in Florida and Kentucky to prepare for the Derby. He was ready for his rival.

Affirmed won the Derby, holding off a determined last effort by Alydar for a one-and-a-half-length victory. The margin was closer in the Preakness, with Affirmed edging out Alydar by a neck. It was a near photo-finish in the Belmont. Affirmed won again, but Alydar was less than a head behind. Some sports fans wished that there could have been two Triple Crown awards given out in 1978. Both horses deserved one. Second-place Alydar could still be proud. His son Alysheba captured the 1987 Derby. Alysheba also won purses of over $6 million in his career—the all-time record.

Steve Cauthen was one of the youngest jockeys ever to race in the Derby.

It is Derby Day in 1989, eleven years after the Affirmed–Alydar rivalry. The track is muddy, but that does not matter to these great horses, their riders, or to the thousands of fans packing Churchill Downs. Easy Goer is the favorite, but some fans believe that Houston or Sunday Silence may upset the big colt.

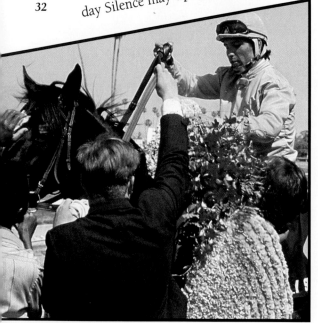

Sunday Silence was the upset winner in 1989.

Houston sets the pace at the half-mile point. Northern Wolf is right behind him, edging closer. Suddenly, as the field of horses reaches the turn, Sunday Silence makes his move, coming up on the outside of the leaders. Easy Goer tries to do the same, but he does not respond to jockey Pat Day. With jockey Pat Valenzuela crouched down as low as possible, Sunday Silence moves in toward the rail so that no other horses will block him or box him in. Surprisingly, there are no other horses in the way. No one is gaining on him.

Then, in the stretch the others increase their speed, with the jockeys cracking their whips. But it is too late. The crowd explodes with thunderous cheering! Easy Goer has been upset, finishing second. Although there are only five lengths between the first eight finishers, Sunday Silence has made history.

He prances proudly to the Winner's Circle to receive the traditional blanket of roses. The 115th Run for the Roses is now over, and Sunday Silence has taken his place in racing history, alongside Hindoo, Black Gold, Whirlaway, Citation, Secretariat, Seattle Slew, and Affirmed. He is a Kentucky Derby winner, horse racing's highest honor.